How Do Children Learn to Use

The Gift of Words

A Conversation Guidebook for Parents and Children
By Talmage M. Steele

This book is dedicated to Eric. We are perfect partners because we are never on the same page; and to Clara and Edie who learned to talk and taught me how they did it.

ISBN 978-1-54393-560-8

My name is **Wallace Quentin Wordsworthy, Jr.**
I will talk anytime, to anyone, anyplace, about
anything. Let's partner up to help these kids learn lots
of words. Kids need a big vocabulary to
succeed in school, at work, and in life.

Before children learn to read, they need to know thousands of words.
This workbook has *reading pages* that explain how children learn words
and it has *talking pages* to develop their vocabulary.

First read how children learn words,
then pick a conversation starter and add
your own delicious words to the pictures.

Let your children talk about the pictures. Take turns.
Let them make up their own stories.

TABLE OF CONTENTS

How does a child learn to talk?

Babies have cells for words in their brains, but…

SOMETHING
IS
MISSING.

Those brain cells need help. Children need a grownup to say the words out loud.
Your child needs you.

Wallace Quentin Wordsworthy, Jr. knows.

This book is not about reading.
It is about talking.
No need to read the book
straight through.
We will Talk! Chat!
Whisper! Gab! Lecture! Shout!
Yammer! Verbalize!

Somebody must give them the words.

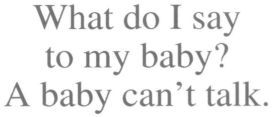

What do I say
to my baby?
A baby can't talk.

Name what he is doing out loud. When he cries, give him the words for what he wants. You don't need fancy words or extra time.

Name what you see.
"You have a dirty diaper."

Words empower a child at school, at work, in life. A child needs a mama to give her a word for everything she sees, touches and does.

Fill this brain with **millions** of words. When she learns to read she will need all of those words.

Just name what you see. It adds up. A big vocabulary is the key to success in school, at work, and at home. It doesn't take more time. It takes more words.

That is a lot of words. I don't think I can say that many.

Get your child. Turn the page.
Pick a conversation starter and talk.

11

It is possible to get out of the door
in 10 words or in 2000 words.
It doesn't take more time.
It takes more words, any words.
1, 2, 3 Say what you see.

Invite Jimmy Over for Talk Time

Jimmy's mama wants him to have the power of a big vocabulary. So Clara's mama was kind enough to invite Jimmy and his mama over for a lot of talk.

Clara put stickers in the book and on herself. Give your child the words. Describe the stickers. Name the places where Clara put the stickers.

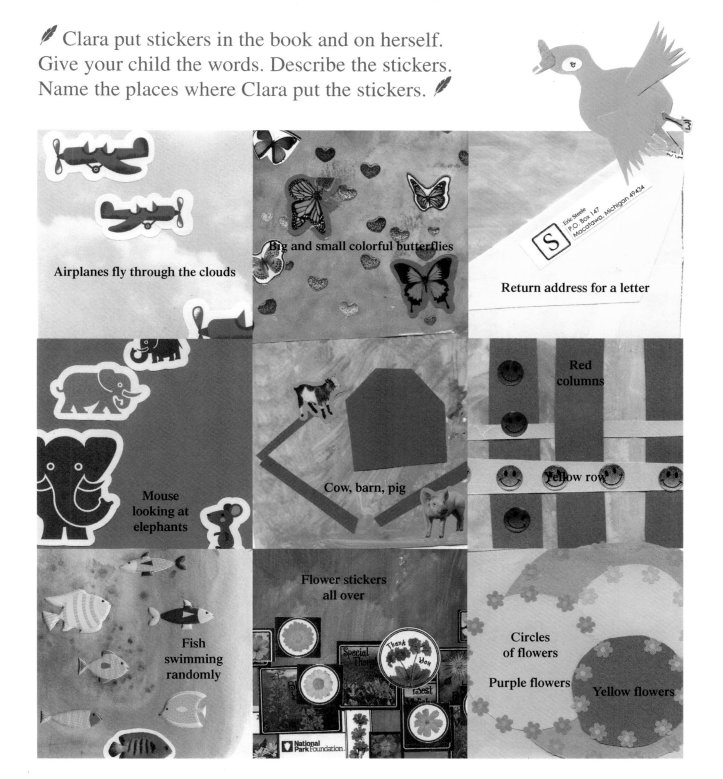

Airplanes fly through the clouds

Big and small colorful butterflies

Return address for a letter

Mouse looking at elephants

Cow, barn, pig

Red columns

Yellow row

Fish swimming randomly

Flower stickers all over

Circles of flowers

Purple flowers

Yellow flowers

Peek-A-Boo with a Mirror

Conversation Starter #5 **A Sticker Hunt**

Where are the heart stickers? Don't point. Use words.

A red sticker is on mama's fingernail.

A rocket sticker is on the balloon.

We all say "stickers" out loud so our brains can hear it.

Sticker, Sticker, Sticker, Sticker, Sticker, Sticker, Sticker, Sticker

Brains take time to remember. Repeat the words. Just keep it fun.

Jimmy wants to know
what is in Clara's
backpack.

Clara's stickers are in her
blue backpack.

Give me sticker
words, Mama!

Jimmy put the rocket shooting
up the door frame.

Place words are
really difficult to
remember.

Clara is sticking
heart stickers on
the front of
her leg.

🖋 Keep talking! 🖋

The flower sticker is behind the chair.

Can you find places to use these words: IN, UP, ON, ACROSS, BETWEEN, UNDER?

The fish sticker is between the chair rollers.

The heart sticker is under the desk.

Smiley face stickers are running across the floor.

21

Conversation Starter #7 **Do the Hokey Pokey**

Put your left knee in
and shake it all about.

Put your right hand in
and shake it all about.

Do the Hokey Pokey and turn yourself around.

22

It is fun to repeat the words in a song. Sing what you see, that's what it's all about.

How else will they know what a knee is?

23

Cook It, Eat It, Clean It Up

Mamas have a lot to say
about each and every food.
Name it.
Taste it.
Smell it.
Heat it. Fry it. Bake it.
Fix it. Stir it. Blend it.
Eat. Talk.
More please. No thank you.
Clean it up.

25

Be Wonder Woman

One step to growing up: **PRETEND.**

Clara wants to be like her mother when she grows up. She wants to be Wonder Woman. Pretending is a great way to learn new words. Her mama can give her the words to pretend to be a grownup.

🪶 Bosses know the most words in the office. In real life, the boss gets to talk the most, because she can.

Say it loud so her brain can hear it. 🪶

Conversation Starter #10

Build a Skyscraper

When Jimmy pretends to go to the construction site, he puts on his hard hat and Clara joins him to build a skyscraper with blocks. Sometimes Jimmy knocks down the building with his backhoe.

It takes a lot of words to run the show.

🖋Because he knows a lot of words, Jimmy knows the names for all the tools and machines. He can teach the others how the tools work. 🖋

Blocks

Hard hat

Skyscraper

Backhoe

Tire

Loving words
welcome everybody home.
Words help soothe
the tiredness
of a long day.

Family talks at night add
kind words to a child's life
in ways no TV program can.

30

A magical moment for storytelling comes every night, tucked in bed with the lights out.

A story can start with
I was really scared today when ...
On the bus, somebody ...
Today I lost ...

A story can end with
They all lived happily ever after.
We can finish this story tomorrow night.
Mama will take care of you.

Children want to see themselves in the story.
Sometimes the best stories start with
Today...
Where were you? What happened? Who did it? How do we feel about that? Why?